Women
WALKING OUT
of the
WILDERNESS

Dr. Angela J. Clark

ISBN 978-1-63630-287-4 (Paperback)
ISBN 978-1-63630-288-1 (Digital)

Covenant Books, Inc.
11661 Hwy 707
Murrells Inlet, SC 29576
www.covenantbooks.com

To my family and friends who have been so supportive.
I am free, no more chains holding me.

IT'S TIME TO LEAVE EGYPT

*P*erhaps we are like the Israelites; the time of departure has come. There's so much chaos around us that we can't seem to think straight and pack. One thing is for sure, when God says, "It's time to go," departure is at hand, no matter what type of bondage we find ourselves in. The moment we cry out to the Lord in our distress, God will raise up a deliverer. People stay in marriages, relationships, churches, and organizations past their season. There's no fruit, no increase, and no signs of life. A dead flower, when immersed in water, will show signs of life after a period. The labor became so intense that the straw used to make bricks was taken away. The people were forced to produce the same quota as before. How is it possible for a marriage to work when both partners won't commit to change? Relationships will fail if the scales of giving and receiving are tipped. When the church allows compromise to the degree it affects the presence of God. Will you forfeit your integrity to remain with an organization that has no values?

Egypt looked good compared to the promised land for these reasons. They were given instructions from Moses to mark their doorpost with the blood of an unblemished lamb. They could only carry enough food for the journey. I encourage every child of God to mark yourself with the blood. Where the blood is applied, the waster and the destroyer can't enter. The night of the Passover, the death angel passed over the Israelites but not the Egyptians' first-born. The enemy's job is to make you think where you are now is your best life. It had to resort to the last plague of death before the Pharaoh would release the children of Israel.

When you give people too much power over your life and they strip you of your resources, that is when you have made flesh your arm. It also can make you very lazy in faith. They were stuck in the mud before Moses came and got in the mud in order to pull them out. Remember, they were making bricks. This was used for building. How long will you build for someone else? Moses had to lead them out mentally before he could lead them physically. A person could have been so emotionally damaged that it can paralyze them. Moses identified himself with the people by working alongside them. This gave him an opportunity to interject the plan for freedom. People don't relate to an individual who appears to have never experienced what they are going through. The phrase now is, "Can you feel me?"

Jochebed, the mother Moses, hid him and sent him down the Nile. His sister was looking from a distance, ensuring that he was found. Later, when the pharaoh's daughter needed a nurse, she was hired. At the appointed time, you will be called from behind the scenes. David was tending sheep and unaware of the dinner with Samuel. They could not be seated until David was brought inside. The part we play in God's plan is so vital that He knows how to involve us. Moses had to see an Egyptian mistreating an Israelite to get involved, only to have his fellow man rebuke him. Everyone will not receive your help. There will be times you will have to take the reins of leadership without permission. Moses ran away for a time from what He should have ran toward. I believe before the curtain is pulled back on our destinies, we must do menial things before we master major things. We are unnoticed before being noticed. This is where the focus is taken off you. These times are called the backside of the mountain.

It takes more than a Bible and a briefcase to lead a group of people. You realize that they are His people and the sheep of His pasture, praying over every aspect of the service, studying at great lengths, and loving them right where they are at. It is in these times of preparation that you discover your strengths and weaknesses. God can use it all to accomplish His mission on earth. The disciples weren't perfect, and neither will we be. Availability is what God needs most of all.

Don't allow your weaknesses to keep you from walking.

Moses was not afraid of leaving the palace or the hard labor of the taskmasters. He was afraid to talk and unsure of what to say.

The enemy's job is to magnify our weaknesses so, we will focus on our inadequacies while your capabilities lie dormant. This is a roadblock that has hindered a many of people from greatness. It affects the female gender to such a degree. They minimize a platform for a place to preach, but their potential is pointing to nations. They will be called evangelists before they submit to apostleship. Identity is a necessary part of who we are. Identification cards are vital for proof of an individual's identity. Identity crisis leads to the misplacement and mismanagement of time, money, and resources. Many people become overachievers resulting in taking positions their character cannot keep them. Know that you are enough. God has equipped you with what you need. Early stages of ministry can be very intense and intimidating. I had been an evangelist for twenty-plus years. I could love them and leave them. Now I was married to a flock, and they needed a shepherd. Injustice angered Moses to such a degree; he took the assignment to lead the Israelites out of bondage. He became aware that it was not going to be an easy task. The people had adjusted themselves to their natural habitation. My passion to see people move out into their calling became a frustration. Potential is that hidden drive that lies dormant until aroused by purpose. Paul encouraged us to fan the flames inside us. Everyone is passionate about something. Everyone, like David, has a cause. Discover this cause and the passion to fight for it will arouse. We all were created for purpose, and there is a quest in every individual to find out what that is. It is the answer to the world problems and the key to many locked doors.

ENOUGH

*T*his is the fork in the road everyone must arrive to in order to move forward. We've made bricks long enough for the pharaoh. There were good and bad pharaohs. Some who knew not Joseph, they won't all be kind. They won't all help you with your dream either, especially when it will cause you to leave them. Joseph was employed by potiphar and was entrusted with all that he had to manage it during the famine. The more responsibility given us should not be allowed to entrap us. There will always be a Potiphar's wife who will lie on you because you won't lie with her. These are times the Lord will vindicate you and restore trust and restore your position. Moses was vindicated before the eyes of the pharaoh. He asked him to let the children of Israel so that they may worship God. Each plague was a ramification for his unwillingness to comply. Earlier, I wrote that one must leave Egypt mentally and physically. Renounce every painful situation that occurred while in bondage. Refuse to vindicate yourself, and allow God to do it. This is easier written than done because it's human nature to retaliate. God has called us to operate by a different standard of rules. You will borrow from your slave masters before you leave Egypt.

The Israelites were instructed to borrow silver and gold. Maybe you will take away ideas and policies you can use. Anything of value, take it with you, because you earned it. This would be a loan that would be defaulted on. They were never returning to Egypt because exodus is a place of no return. Due diligence is when something rightfully owed is given back to the owner. Many people who were supposed to be a blessing to you, but they kept back what was due. Good news, our God is a master at due diligence. People make the mistake of leaving a former job before learning all they can. Those are the times you need the jaws of a chipmunk. They pack them full and save the food for the winter. It is the wise who gain knowledge from every place they go.

PREPARATION FOR THE EXODUS

I was standing in my kitchen packaging vegetables for cooking, and it reminded me of the instructions given to the children of Israel. Moses told them what kind of food to prepare, how much to bring, and how to pack it. They did not need a Yeti cooler of food because of the journey; it would have slowed them down. What and who are you trying to take with you that will slow you down? The Lord will sustain you if He sends you. He wanted them to know him as a provider, protector and a Pathfinder. I may be talking to my reader and you're saying, "I'm stuck in the middle of this wilderness, and the forest of indecision is in front of me." God is equipped for those situations, and He is equipping you in them. He promised to make the crooked places straight, the rough places smooth, the valleys exalted, and the mountains made low so His children can come across. Let's pack and leave Egypt. God is going to show us some amazing feats as we journey forward. You will never know until you go.

We live with too many regrets: what if, I should have, maybe, or will it work? You will never know the answer to these questions if you don't try. Someone is always watching you, and your success could be the catapult of someone else's success. If you are not motivated to do it for you, be a success for the rest of us. We have a great cloud of witnesses cheering us on from the heavenly grandstands. They succeeded, and so will you. They had strengths and weaknesses as well. This was to be an example. God doesn't call the perfect. He calls us in our present condition and perfects us for His use. David and Sampson had flesh problems. Gideon and Elijah were afraid. Abraham and Moses were unsure. This did not stop God from choosing them.

Stop watching from the grandstands of life, and start walking where other men have sank. Peter got out of the boat and started walking toward Jesus. He is bidding you to come. All you need is one word from God.

LET MY PEOPLE GO

*L*etting go is never an easy task but not difficult when both parties agree. Moses's assignment was to go and tell the pharaoh to let the people go, that they may worship God. It seems like a request that wouldn't be refused. The moment people are viewed as a commodity and not a compliment to your assignment, one could easily fall into ownership default. This is when you forget who the people belong to. You begin to want control over God's heritage, and He in turn will remind you of your position. People would rather hang on to best and never experience better. Revenue was the pharaoh's problem, and it's like that today in the church. People come to our church with gifts and talents. Status nor wealth should never determine how people are treated. The Bible says they should be treated no differently. Sadly, in most cases they are given preferential treatment. This is the biggest mistake any leader can do. Train them all because they may have knowledge, but they don't come in the door knowing your vision. Faithfulness and consistency are character builders.

The Israelites worked every day under harsh conditions but remained faithful. Both parties struggled with letting go; after leaving, they constantly referred to Egypt. People hate to leave their comfort zones; here they don't have to change. They will remain the same if never challenged. It is my opinion that most of us get discouraged with the promised land because it is undeveloped. We want things already prepared and ready for use. The word of God says we must plant and build for ourselves. Adam was put in the garden of Eden, but he had to name the animals and be fruitful and multiply. Adam had some work to do; God's part was done.

The purpose of the exodus was to allow the Israelites to freely worship. Don't focus so much on your destination that you forget what you were destined for.

PROBLEM PEOPLE

*P*rominent people should never become a problem. They are only an adviser, Godly wisdom is advisable but is never to replace God. Many people get disappointed with these people because they may have wisdom. They are not all-knowing, and they have their own set of problems to deal with. God is jealous; he'll have no other God before him. We must keep everything in perspective; always respect and honor those in authority.

"Look to the hills from which cometh your help, all your help cometh from the Lord." This person will make your life for the better, but keep them in their proper place. There will always be pharaohs, so don't be moved by them. Move with them instead. Obey them who have rule over you, whether they are harsh or kind. I worked in healthcare for twenty years plus, and in that time frame, leadership changed numerous times. The change brought in new systems and paperwork. Obedience never changes because of a change of leadership. It only changes when the person resists change and refuses to comply. God called us to change. Why is it when people encounter change, we grumble and complain?

Moses led people who resisted and questioned everything he did. This only made the job harder and the journey longer. When there's a problem, God will always raise up a leader in the event of a crisis. We all are called to solve some type of problem. Plumbers, firemen, doctors, lawyers are all problem-solvers. Schools are started to solve the education problem. We can't make people learn, but we can make provision for them to get the tools needed. Moses could not make these people follow him. Who knows, like Esther, were you brought to the kingdom for such a time as this? The hand you were dealt with is a winning hand. It's all in how you play the cards you were dealt. The promised land is for problem people also. Be the solution and not the problem.

WHERE YOU CAME FROM COULD BE WHAT YOU'RE CALLED TO

I remember my childhood being reared by my elderly great-grandmother. She was very strict, and I only could go to church and school. I wanted to do things I saw other kids participate in. I felt like I was tied to a post like the colt. Times like these, we question and feel forgotten; but this is farther from the truth. God is developing you in His dark room. I became an avid reader and writer. The church experience was the classroom, where I learned church structure. I became acquainted with prayer and church people. Today, I'm not shocked of what happens in church because I've seen it before. I vividly remember the church voting a pastor out of office. This is where I heard for the first time, "Dust your feet if peace is not in a house you entered."

The pastor and his family left that church and moved away. His kids were the only playmates I had on the street. Later, his son became a pastor himself. I'm sure her remembered the pitfalls in ministry from his earlier experience. They installed a new pastor. As a child, I didn't have a good feeling about this decision. I was a child, and no one would listen to me. God can deal with you as a child for your future as an adult. He did it with Samuel, and he learned to know and obey the voice of God. I saw this same pastor as an adult in Gainesville Hospital. He was very ill. I acknowledged him and told him who my relatives were and that I was under his leadership as a child. This is where you need the spirit of discernment so that you won't follow the wrong person. Everyone you meet is not your Moses, and I have seen too many people follow individuals who do not pour into them for their purpose. Moses went from his mother's hands to the pharaoh's daughter's hands back to his mother's hands. Trust God to hand you over to the right people. Deal with the hand you are dealt. Play to win the game.

FEW WILL WALK DOWN
THE ROAD TO FREEDOM

I guess by now, you see that I refer to Moses and other characters of the Bible. I will also interject personal stories of my own. This is the very roadmap that was my compass to my exodus. I must tell it in the order I experienced it so that each moment is captured for the next person who is ready to walk out of the wilderness. They, too, will understand these occurrences will confront you also. The children of Israel were led out by instructions given to Moses by God. Moses was a meek man. This is a fruit that should mark every true leader. It is needed to withstand the pressures and demands put upon you by the people. They have silent demands, doubt, worry, and fear. They scream at a leader, and when he is unsure of himself, he will succumb to the demands and compromise.

Present yourself as confident in public; go to God privately with fears and doubts. You are going to have these days, and all leaders are not superheroes with an *S* on their chests. A true leader can't stand to see people hurting. This is what provoked Moses, and this is what should provoke you to see the condition of humanity. Jesus was sent as a substitute because of our condition. God didn't want us to remain in the shape that the world was in. This will cause you to fast and pray for people. Seek out information and strategies in which you can help an individual. Jesus was moved with compassion when He went from place to place. If you will serve from this place, you will witness the hand of God move impossible situations for people. In times of a storm, God will see your condition and send someone to your aid. Who can find a man who will stand in the gap and make up the hedge? Send me, Lord, I'll go.

Moses was the man for the assignment, and so are you. Meekness doesn't mean you are weak, but on the contrary, hold fast to your convictions. No matter how the people grumbled, mumbled, and complained, Moses kept walking. This is what leaders must show the people in order to keep movement. We can't allow everything to stop us and expect people to follow us. They will be stopping and starting all the time. Moses was not leading a football team; he was leading millions to freedom. The size of the people is not the factor; it's your ability to get them to their destiny, which is their destination. Some will not know where they are headed; these are the ones who will stay with you until they get clarity. There are a number who's been called to stay, and they are loyal. Those are who, in time, will carry on and lead. Everyone who started with Moses didn't finish with him; some died in the wilderness from disobedience. Moses had to keep it moving. Walking involves more than a movement of your legs; it has a mindset one must possess in order to continue in the faith.

A sailor is at sea, and a storm arises. He throws out an anchor to hold the ship in place. We, too, must have our faith anchored in the Lord. Romans 8 states, "Don't let anyone drive a wedge between us and Christ's love for us." Not trouble, not hard times, not hatred, not hunger, not homelessness, not bullying threats, not backstabbing, not even the worst sins listed in scripture. Life is a journey, and I have been delayed in getting to my destination by fatal distractions and good time detours.

In those times, stop and pause for a minute and say, "Lord, where do I go from here?"

Acknowledge Him in all your ways, and He will direct your path.

The journey is your assignment. Remember the people are only a small piece of the puzzle. People are given choices in life to follow or falter. A leader has no control over a person's free will. God won't take the ability to make choices from us. Instruct them with the instructions handed down to you as clear as you can articulate them. You as their leader should be first partaker in following through with an assignment, then others will follow along. "Ye are our epistle written in our hearts known and read of all men" (2 Cor. 3:2 KJV). You cannot stop people from watching you, but you can control what they see. You will face numerous pharaohs for the people you are responsible to lead. Leaders take the brunt of verbal and physical abuse on behalf of the people. You will get denials and rejections that your congregation and family may never know about. It's almost as if you were in a boxing match; every round gets more intense. The blows can leave each opponent blinded. Know that a winner is in that ring. The people you are called to lead are depending on you to be Rocky.

God calls, glorifies, and equips for each assignment. Everyone is not called to lead everyone; you will see fruit over time if the job is done according to plan. Satan comes to steal, kill, and destroy. He wants to win using unfair tactics on God's people. Jesus won over two thousand years ago, and we are still winning. Goodness and mercy follows us everywhere we go, so we are not at the mercy of anyone. God never asks you to do anything alone. He never leaves us or forsakes us. He promised to be with us to the end of the age. I've seen God show up for me when I was at my wit's end. He still parts the Red Sea of adversity today. It's those times that things he told you begin to make sense. The burning bush encounter revealed the realness of God to Moses. Taking off your shoes can only lead you down the proper path that is laid out for you. Footprints are still in the sand, and there is only one set because He's carrying you.

DESTINED AND DESIGNED
FOR THE ASSIGNMENT

People who you are made to lead can also make you into the person God designed. Destined from birth, Moses was assigned to lead a great nation. Jeremiah had to prophesy and not become a popular person with the people. This will form you if you are out of shape in any capacity. It sounds so exciting when we receive a prophetic word that we have been called. If the person is not careful, it can make them run out before time. Premature advancement is dangerous and could kill your vision and cause you to miscarriage.

Callings can be like baking cakes. If one ingredient is missing, it will be evident that it is not ready. Taking it from the oven too soon will cause the cake to fall. People can't be saved from every dilemma or they will never know how to suffer. Calling without character is charisma only. The church has enough of that in this dispensation. Moses's character was developed on the backside of a mountain, his experience in the wilderness, and his feat at the Red Sea.

Accountability is something you will get used to dealing with because you will be held at a higher standard for being a leader. Too much is given, much is required. Moses became frustrated, angry, tired, and unsure. All of these were listed as weaknesses, but he never turned away from his assignment.

Paul asked God thrice to take away the thorn from his flesh, but after it didn't happen, he depended on the grace of God to help him do his God-given assignment. I have had these same emotions in my tenure as a pastor; quitting has never been an option. I know God uses imperfect people to carry out His perfect will. Deep in all our core being, we desire to please God. Things may not always go as planned. God can change our plans and still manage to fit us into them. Our ways are not His ways, neither are our thoughts His thoughts.

HURRY UP

God does not always move at a slow pace. The Israelites had to leave in haste when they left Egypt. Moses had to get all those people out in a hurry. What a big responsibility for one man, but he was not alone. There is not one person I know who doesn't want more. The problem is they don't want more responsibility. I was an evangelist for years, and I could love them and leave them. I became responsible for the most valuable thing God owns, his people.

Most was the responsibility for the provision, protection, and the path of these people. Jehovah Shammah was with them, and He still is with us. I started the first church in a nightclub. The building was used for dog fights after being abandoned for years. I remember the stench of urine and manure that was in that building. My husband and I got a shovel and gloves and started to pick it up. I heard inside, "This is going to be the condition of some of the people's lives. Can I trust you with them? This is the kind of people I'm giving you to lead. Will you do it?"

I said within myself, yes, to the Lord; and we started that ministry on an Easter Sunday. I received a grant to take homecooked meals from a local restaurant to the elderly in the community. We would have church; a driver would be assigned to pick up the food weekly. The other members would assist in serving and delivering the dinners. The ministry had a clothing pantry, and the people bought us out when I sold every item for a dollar. They would not take the clothing for free.

We had to hurry to get this done every Sunday, but it happened. People will follow you at a fast or slow pace. Just lead them, and they will follow.

YOU DON'T ALWAYS HAVE
TO LEAVE TO LEAD

I won't assume every reader had to leave to lead. When you have maxed out in every capacity of leadership. This is when you have taken every opportunity given to you in your present position and produced more. People normally give their pastors, bosses, and others just enough. These people normally only go as far as the level of service they are willing to give. Moses had to leave the palace in order to identify with his new congregation in the mud pit. He probably had a nice room, the best of foods, and several servants at his beck and call. He refused to be called the pharaoh's daughter's son. Be careful who you identify with.

The place where God starts you may not be glamorous, and you may not know anyone; it's called new beginnings. God will cause you to speak into existence everything you need by faith. Oh, the joy of watching the manifestation unfold as you walk by faith and not by sight.

My first congregation consisted of myself and my husband. The church was set up for service, and we arrived on time with the expectation that He would meet us there. Eleven years later, I still show up on time, and I still expect Him to show up. This was sixty-plus members later. Guests would come to our first location, but they had no commitment. I served them as members by faith, so I would be prepared for future members. The first design was four dining room tables because it was going to be a mission outreach to feed the people. The Lord wanted me to feed His sheep. I was so proud of this place; I kept it shiny and clean because I wanted to be a good steward of what God had given me. I desired to do things in an excellent spirit. The promises of God are yes and amen. I believe all we want is the yes, but in the amen (so be it) is the agreement with God in the situations He puts us in. I thought we would be packed out every Sunday and everyone would understand the calling on my life. Reality set in, and in these times, you must have to lead. You will experience better people, lasting memories, and good times. Moses's speech impediment might have seemed as though it was a hindrance, but on the contrary, it allowed his brother Aaron to come alongside him. Everyone needs an Aaron and Hur in this world; they were put there to hold your arms. They must be allowed to do their job.

I have found it is easier to talk about what you will do than do what you talk about. The dictionary describes this type of person as a procrastinator. I would often talk about the day I would be in full-time ministry. I'm sure when I left their presence, I was the topic of conversation. The moment you decide to step out of the boat, you rock the boat. Today I have many coworkers who come to the ministry and see what I said. I remember the exodus from the job like it was yesterday. We were three days into the state inspection, and the workload was very intense. Supervising the Environmental Service Department, which consists of three entities. Too much is given, much is required.

On prior months, I had undergone two major surgeries. I couldn't even take a lunch break because of the constant demands of each day. There was some heavy lifting involved that I wasn't supposed to do. Each day I was faced with a new challenge. I became physically and spiritually weak. I still had the newly launched church on weekends as well. I, too, have faced a Red Sea in front of me and pharaoh's army behind me. I later learned a valuable lesson about sharing your plans with everyone. I had a Judas, and just like for Jesus, he pushed Him to his purpose. Judas hung himself, and so will anyone with wrong motives. There is a song "Smiling Faces" which implies about backstabbers as Judas was to Jesus.

I had to pick up a disaster manual that was updated. This would afford me a lunch break and time to gather my thoughts. I was going to my office to get my keys and overheard a conversation by two men

I thought were inspectors but really was the new cleaning company that was taking over. It was when I got in my car and cried out to God that I was ready to go. The manual was approved, and I was able to pick up some lunch. Before I reentered the building, I heard the answer to my prayer. "Angela, tell him you resign. This is your last day, last hour." I called my husband and discussed it with him.

He said, "Well, come home."

I handed over the approved manual to my administrator. He was relieved that this would not be an issue. I would normally have all my floors done for inspection, but one of my employees was ill.

I told my boss, and he replied, "You need to think about this. We are in the middle of an inspection."

I explained that I had, and my health was declining, and I had made my decision. I put my phone and keys on his desk. I went upstairs and told that friend I was leaving. My only regret was leaving a legacy of no deficiencies. I had nothing left to give. This is key in anything in life when you have nothing left to give. Then you will no longer love it nor will you have the drive to do it as unto the Lord. I was more concerned about my level of service than getting a handsome salary for what I could no longer give. It wasn't a week had gone by that the friend applied for the job. I was asked to help them with the schedule. I told them to follow the existing one until it ran out.

Young upcoming ministers, it may look easy what that senior pastor does until you walk in their shoes. Moses had many people challenge his authority while in the wilderness. They murmured and complained about food, water, and the journey. Each time, He silenced them by being the provision they needed for every situation. I saw Him do the same thing for me—silenced the naysayers as He provided for me starting the very day I left that job. I truly know what it means to step out by faith. The church could not pay me a salary; I had no retirement or savings. My husband had just retired after forty-eight years. That was our income. I had no health insurance, and the vacation time I had was forfeited because of my instant resignation.

I left work that day with the uncertainty that no one ever wants to feel, but I knew that I had to go. I knew that God would provide for me no matter what. I was doing a wedding at that time, so I stopped to the bridal store to make a payment. The owner noticed the countenance on my face, just like Nehemiah's countenance was noticed when he was grieved about the walls of Jerusalem being torn down. She asked me what was wrong, and I proceeded to tell her that I had just resigned from my job. I knew that I had a call from God to go into full-time ministry. I made the payment, and she was about to close her register when she went inside and handed me $200. She told me, "I came to America with a dream and it has come to pass. Angela, I want you to go on and start that church knowing it will come to pass. I'm sowing the seed in your life so that you do what you're supposed to do."

The encouragement that the owner of the bridal store had shown me replayed in my head as I arrived at the nursing facility. The friend I mentioned earlier was here for rehabilitation. The next turn of events made me want to reconsider my resignation. I could not look back; it was up to me to go forward. As I started driving to the nursing home, my car began to act up, and it almost stalled on me. That was when I noticed that my oil gauge was telling me my oil was low. I didn't know about cars, but there was a homeless man standing on the side of the road.

"Can I assist you, ma'am?"

I told him what the car was doing. He looked under the hood and added some oil to the car. He said, "As soon as you get home, park it and call the dealership so you can get a diagnostic test done."

I went to the nursing home to visit my friend, trying to hide my emotions because she had just undergone heart surgery. She did not need to worry nor did she need to be upset. I held back the tears; eventually I did tell her that I had resigned. She took it very well. She said, "I know, it's time for you to go." Little did I know that it was time for both of us to go and for us to exodus. We had to see if we did have the faith in God that we talked about. You step out on God's word, and that's all you must stand on. Her daughter was working at the time of her release from rehab. I became her nurse so that I could assist with her recovery.

God knows what we need in the times of trouble, and he sends us the right help at the right time. I took my car to the dealership for an estimate amount it would cost to get it fixed and what was wrong with the vehicle. I said, "What shall I do, Lord?"

I had a coworker who was a manager in the kitchen. He had just undergone a tragic death of one of his family members. Time and prayer and giving people space is the best thing to do when you don't know what to say. It's just good to be there for them, letting them know that you care. He contacted me after I had left and asked if he could meet me at Starbucks. He said to me, "I came to Florida to be a full-time minister and attend seminary school." He would then go into full-time ministry. He changed his plans and didn't pursue his path. He saw that I was doing what he didn't do, so he began to invest encouragement and financially into my life and ministry. I always told my congregation to always make a list of the debts you owe because you never know when God will tell somebody to use their power and ability to bless you. That seemed farfetched for some people because they didn't believe that God could do such a miraculous thing. Someone pays your debt off and expects nothing in return. Remember, I also had a mortgage to pay; I was able to settle that as well. I put my personal fleece out to the Lord. If he wanted me to go into full-time ministry, He would certainly have to do something about my mortgage. God still works miracles, and if He gave you the vision, he could bring the provision. Trust Him when you can't trace Him.

Once again, He came on the scene and parted a Red Sea for me. The mortgage was behind me, but uncertainty was the haunting feeling awaiting me, but He parted the way. I have walked from one exodus to another. I said during my story you would hear me talk about many things that God has brought me out of. Some of those things you may identify with, some of these things you have not. Keep living. Life causes these things to come about; uncertainties will come up in our lives, but one thing I am certain of is God never changes, and He never wavers, and His word is true. When He promised that He is a Shepherd and we shall not want, He really does mean that.

When He promised that He would never leave us nor would He forsake us, that is true. Would he promise and not perform it? He is not like man nor the son of man that he has to repent. If he said it, He'll do it; if He spoke it, He'll make it good. He is not lying to you; every word of God is true. The car and the house were just symbols of natural things there were spiritual adjustments about to occur in my life. I was out of oil and overdrawn. I needed to be debt-free by forgiveness from others and God. I got a printout on my life and began to take inventory on my life. I had been with those people for over twenty years, so it was like family. Family will hurt you, and you can also hurt them. I was in desperate need of inner and outer healing.

One morning in my prayer time, I was praying about the pain in my hips. I was taking injections as a remedy. The Lord answered me, "Angela, forgive your staff, and I'll heal your hips." After I resigned, I was told of the betrayal of many of them whom I had extended favor to. People are prone to do this when afraid, so don't take offense like I did. They call it saving your own skin. God was about to do the same open-heart surgery on me as the doctors had performed on my friend.

Not everyone who starts on this journey with you would make it to the destination with you. Moses did not make it to the destination with the children of Israel. He saw the promised land, but he never did enter it. I also lost a great friend and a mentor during this time. I thought that they would be here to see the new church, to view the new land.

I recall my weakest point as a babe in Christ when I had been delivered from crack cocaine, and I really was having the urge to go back. I knew that if I went back at that time, I probably would never have returned. This person allowed me to sit under their garage and just talk for hours and hours and bear my soul. I could go back and begin this journey again. We all need someone in our lives who is stronger than us, that at our weakest points they can bear the infirmity of the weak. The Bible declares that the strong should bear the infirmity of the weak. I can say that I'm standing as a senior pastor of a church because this person thought it not robbery to take time with me so that I would not go back. Will you also be that Moses for someone? Will you be their mentor until you see them walk in their deliverance? They may have never seen it if in your strongest time you helped them in their weakest times. I found that accountability is one thing that we all need when you are a person of destiny. A leader needs to be accountable to someone speaking in your life—someone praying for you, someone who supports you. I had this person in my life all through my beginnings when I had an evangelistic team. We were on the team together, but she never thought it robbery to see me or anyone go on to the next level. You need someone in your life who's not jealous of your next level; that is the person who would be your Aaron and Hur. The next chapter of my life, I would never forget this faithful warrior, and she will always be in my heart. I know that she's among those great clouds of witnesses right now cheering me on, saying, "Angie, you can do it."

GO AHEAD

*Y*ou need to do it for all the women who are in the clergy that are coming, for the clergy that are leaving the clergy. I want you to think about it before you leave; don't go out empty. God has an assignment for your hands. Maybe it's not behind the pulpit; maybe it's in domestic violence. Maybe it's with orphanages or pro-life or in the White House or in the prisons. Wherever it is, your voice needs to be heard. You are the Deborah who those people need to sit under the tree with and be able to come to you for the wisdom that God has put on the inside of you. I'm telling you from my heart, don't give up, woman of God. Don't give up, man of God. Don't give in, missionary, things will get better. Resources and finances will come for your vision. Don't give up on God because He won't give up on you.

We have been called to bring reconciliation, reconciling man back to God. We are his feet, his hands, and his mouthpiece on earth. "Go ye therefore, and teach all nations, baptizing them in the name of the Father and of the Son, and of the Holy Ghost (Matt 28:19 KJV). We are not alone in this thing. He is with us. He had never left us. I implore you as you read this book to go on and not to drop out of the race. "The race is not given to the swift nor the strong but he who endures until the end" (Eccles. 9:11).

Jesus and Moses were known as the meekest men in the Bible; their meekness was not associated with weakness at all. Jesus turned over the tables in the temple because of buying and selling. He said his house shall be called a house of prayer, but it had become a den of thieves. Moses come down from Sinai in the presence of the Almighty with the Ten Commandments in hand and dropped them and shattered the stone into many pieces because while he was away, the people formed a golden calf. What set these men apart to be classified as the meekest men in the Bible? They knew the art of ministry of the towel: Jesus taught this lesson to his disciples as he washed their feet. Peter didn't think he was worthy. Jesus assured him that if he didn't allow it, he would have no part of him.

Servanthood was their outstanding trait above all; they loved and served the people who followed them. We can't serve people we don't love. You can't love without serving. They both go hand in hand. You must know when the towel is used, it may never be used on you. If the people are self-centered, you will never be in the center. Therefore, don't be weary in doing well, for you will reap in due season if you don't faint. Moses fainted, and he did not reach the promised land with his chosen people. He struck the rock instead of speaking to it. Moses allowed the people's pressure to affect his progress. If you are going to walk out of any wilderness situation, this is something you cannot allow. Pressure will cause you to blow; it's no different than a pressure cooker. The pot is designed to cook the contents at a faster rate. The instructions warn you not to take the lid off before a time because it can cause you potential harm. Pressure from people whom you lead can cause you to take the lid off your vision before a certain period. The people got the promise of the water; it came gushing out of the rock. Moses, on the other hand, missed the promised land because of it. He could view it only.

I can attest to this. In earlier years of ministry, I wanted everybody to like me. I desired to see the church overflowing with people and everyone unified, doing the work of the kingdom. I soon came to realize you can go above and beyond for people, but it may not come into fruition until years. Nobody is given an assignment by God without a manual of instructions. All the pages may not be in there at first. This is so you can add more information as is given. There will also be pages of your life that must be removed. Remove the chapter of yesteryears. Whatever you hold on to makes it harder to leave Egypt. Remember, their whole mentality while heading to the promised land was to reflect. In my lifetime, God has worked miracles, parted many Red Seas for me and so forth. I know there is more. If you don't keep this mindset, you will pitch a tent and settle. Dust is one of the things that settles. We came from dust; the Word says we will return to the dust. Don't you get so comfortable that you pitch a tent in the wilderness. People of this mindset are predictable, prejudice, and can pose to be a big problem on the journey. Literally, they will slow down the progress of everything you are trying to do. Moses became frustrated because he had people who were tired of walking and just wanted to settle. There will be people among you who just want to sit, watch, and criticize others who are advancing. They are the ones who have been put on the bench by the coach, God Himself.

Even in childbirth there was an exodus. The baby is connected to the umbilical cord, which gives it nourishment it needs to survive. After a nine-month period, it's time to cut the cord. God does the same; He allows us to be connected to certain people, things and places for a season. When the cord is cut, then your life support comes from Him alone. He can show Himself to be every one of His great names in most difficult times. We as a people of God can have full assurance that as "He said to his servants, stay here with the donkey while I and the boy go over there. We will worship and then we will come back to you" (Gen. 22:5). He didn't know how God would provide, but he knew that he would. God has a ram in the bush; this is an alternative way to get the job done. Despite all the children of Israel faced, God always provided what they needed. Moses would be cut, and he would no longer be with them. God had another plan for a successor, Joshua, who was put into place for them. Our God never runs out of solutions. Trust, depend, and rely on Him. He will never fail you.

PROCEED

Proceed is a word that defines movement. *Move forward* is written in the fabric of this word. Make this your mission statement. Become focused on your God-given destiny. Problems will emerge to stop you from proceeding. I want to plead with my audience of readers, don't stop in the middle of the wilderness; proceed and follow the leader. There are going to be some days when the heat may be turned up. There are going to be some cold nights; cover yourself. We all get tired of walking sometimes; pitch a tent. Parking is not an option when you are proceeding. Parking meters run out of time, and a person is fined after a long period of time. Don't miss the timing of God. You can stay in a place to long and end up like Lot's wife a monument instead of a movement. Miriam and Aaron disagreed with Moses about his wife. When leading people out of something they had gotten accustomed to, expect opposition. We expect it from our enemies and nonrelated people, but from within, it is always a major distraction.

The Word declares the Lord's eyes roam, discerning both the good and the evil. People don't realize that the Lord knows. Today with social media (Twitter, Instagram, etc.), and television, people tend to voice suppressed feelings and opinions rather than convey the message to whom it is intended. This is exactly what Miriam and Aaron did. They discussed among themselves of their objection to Moses's wife being of another nationality. Regardless of the subject matter, people would rather form an opinion than go to the horse for the source. The Lord hears this conversation and imposes leprosy on them both. And those days, when you have leprosy, you were marked unclean and had to be removed from the population until healed. The priest had to declare you clean for you to return into the camp.

Aaron and Miriam learned a valuable lesson about speaking against a leader. We don't have to agree with decision made by a leader, but there would be less disageement if we go to them for understanding. Ask Him to deal with this person. Ask God to give you the opportune time to talk to them. Moses never had this problem again, period. God dealt with the matter for him. You won't have to fight every battle and you won't know every opposing person. God knows it's good for us not to know all our opposers so we can continue loving and leading them.

People are focused at times on the problem, until they can't see the answer when it arrives. Moses was the answer that the children of Israel prayed for. God raises up deliverers, and they don't necessarily have to fit our description of what they should be. God takes the foolish things of this world to confound the wise. The Father knows best. He could have chosen the most eloquent speaker and someone who was confident. Sometimes when people have it all together, they think that their own abilities caused them to succeed. God loves for us to depend on Him. Trust the treasure inside your earthen vessels, but the excellency is of God and not of us. We can marvel at His handiwork. We are His instruments in the hand of a mighty warrior. Our job is to be willing and obedient to the master's plan. His plans for us are good and not evil to give us a future and hope.

AT THE TOP

There's a saying, it's lonely at the top. This is true when it comes to leadership. That's why it's vital to have a personal relationship with God. Leaders need to dialogue because of the multitude of responsibilities given to them. I can see why Moses needed a companion, a person who was indirectly involved with the people. She was supportive of her husband and leader. I'm sure she heard the conversations about her ethnic background. I have a mate who has the most positive outlook on life. If I have a day that may be overwhelming, he doesn't allow it to affect him. He is a good listener and doesn't answer anything quickly. I admit, this frustrates me. God really gave me who I needed to balance me out. If you are reading this book and have multiple tasks or responsibilities, take a moment and stop. Step outside the camp in order to keep your sanity and good name. I recently started taking the day off during the week. I don't do anything concerning ministry. I have a date night with my husband quarterly; I spend time with my kids whether by phone or in person. I take care of my elderly parent, so we have a breakfast date on her monthly doctors' appointments.

I just recently did something out of the box for me: I drove four hours to celebrate a good friend's birthday. I took the liberty to order the meal and her dessert. She arrived at about seven o'clock; the waitress began to bring out the meal items. I told her that I found out cheesecake was her favorite dessert. It was a joy to see her relax and love the choices I made for her. It reminded me of the things I never asked for, but it's the Father's good pleasure to give us the kingdom. We talked and shared about her day. The table behind us had some problems with a drink order. They were being very abrupt and frankly rude. The manager tried to oblige them but to no avail. They proceeded to leave, and when passing our table, the wife made a racist remark. We just smiled and told the manager about the remark. Our dinner was discounted.

We can allow bad breaks to break us, or we can get a breakthrough from what was sent to break us down. Remember I said leaders get lonely in those times; be very careful who you lay your head in their lap. It could be a Delilah spirit who only wanted to know where your strength lies. Never lean on a pole under pressure that's not proven to stay grounded. Many times, we put our trust in people who cannot handle their own problems, and they're trying to take on yours. All you can do to test whether you should trust a person's wisdom is to see how they apply their wisdom to their own lives. These are times when we must put our trust in God.

The Bible tells us some trust in horses, some trust in princes; but I would trust in the name of the Lord. You will also find out as a leader that you will have others around you that are loyal, skeptical and doubtful. Utilize them all in different capacities. Those who truly have your heart will receive your mantle. You can't look at them or even listen to them and tell whether or not they truly have your heart. All you can do as a leader is sit back and watch their actions after a period over time. Time has a way of eating at the core of us and revealing our hearts. Impatient people leave you over time. Complainers will criticize your every move over time. Doubters will use selected hearing mechanisms and stay with you over time. They tune out what they don't want to hear. Whisperers will gossip about you with others. Loyal people will have gotten to know you over time and realize you're a leader and not God. Character development is a necessity if you aspire to be a leader that make a difference. People will test your temperament. You may say I'm easy-going and it takes a lot for me to get mad. You will find yourself some days cussing like Peter. There will be things the Lord will reveal to you that will hurt the very core of your heart. Praying constantly for them at times when you want to rest will become your priority. I wanted to be a leader despite the great cost. Earlier I mentioned this was my career in the natural and spiritual.

Training and more training is all it takes for a person to reign in life; they just need a teachable spirit. Jesus taught the disciples they had questions and He had answers. Much of what they were taught wasn't used until later after He was ascended. Moses knew the way, and the people were to follow him. If your leader has a fifth-grade education and you have a PhD, there's something God put in them that sets you apart. I've had many natural leaders on jobs, but I learned a valuable lesson from each of them. I've only had four spiritual leaders. One taught me how to live, the other to give, the other to love, and the last to pray. I'm grateful for all the life lessons. I sometimes thought I knew more and sized myself up with them, only to find I was a midget in the spirit compared to them.

OPPRESSION

Oppression comes to do just what it was designed to do: oppress the individual and not enable them to rise. Thanks be to God, no amount of weight can hold you down when you allow him to take charge. We in ourselves can't handle the many things we face, but I know someone who two thousand years ago bared a cross that He couldn't carry. Someone assisted Him with the cross. There is assistance for us when you find yourself in this season. It is very important what you say within yourself. Speak the word in any situation. The Shunammite woman had the son, but he later died. She went back to the man of God for help. The prophet sensed something was wrong. He sent his servant to meet her and he asked, "What's wrong"? Her answer was "All is Well".

You see, the woman knew that she could't just sit there and not do nothing. For her situation to change, she had to go back to source. Every time Israel found themselves oppressed, they had left their source, which was God. He had to raise up a deliverer to lift the oppression. She went back to the prophet who told her, "About this time next year, you will have a son." Elijah returned home with the woman and stretched prostrate over her son and breathed into his mouth. Life came back into his body.

God is about to breathe new life on some dead situations. I declare and decree it in Jesus's name. There can be no compromise, for there to be an Exodus. Moses was not going to Him with an ultimatum. Then the Lord said to Moses, "Go to Pharaoh and say to him, this is what the Lord says, 'Let my people go, so that they may worship me.'" (Exod.8:l) Pharaoh knew if he allowed them to go, they weren't coming back. This is what happens to many of God's people when they are brought out of the wilderness situation. They go back, and in that moment, they're enslaved all over again. You will never thrive in the promised land with an Egyptian mentality.

I have made a lot of poor decisions that have had me in debt. I have also been at the door of foreclosure and the ramifications of bankruptcy. These were true wilderness times for me, but God had enrolled me in the school of life. The choices I made were the ones I had to live with. This taught me more than Him telling me what to do. Now I don't have a problem saying, I choose life and life more abundantly. I won't compromise when it comes to doing things in excellence. Somethings are worth the wait. It doesn't have to take forever to have ownership of something, and credit doesn't always have to be an option. A borrower is a slave to the lender.

KNOW WHO'S ON YOUR SHIP

There will be people sent in your life only for information and not a relationship. It's a Delilah spirit, and only through discernment will you know. True relationships last over years and must be tested in the fire of affliction. I'm the type of person who goes the extra mile in a relationship. It's rare that you will find someone who will reciprocate in that manner with you. The initiator should be the reciprocator sometimes. Family, friends, and coworkers need to show love to one another. We are the answers to one another's prayers. Evaluate each relationship, and look for underlying abuse. People can manipulate you; use empathy and false information. Souls ties are formed when you allow people to influence your life to a point that they affect your decisions. Emotions that are damaged are in need of a healing. Healing is necessary, or a plague can spread throughout a camp, home, church, or business.

God is close to the brokenhearted. Put you heart in His hands, and He will protect it well. Miriam and Aaron were let back in the camp after a time of purification. We are predestined. God already knows who will betray us, lie on us, and plot against us. This doesn't surprise God when this happens. He wants us to mature to a level that it doesn't surprise us either. I found myself wasting too much time chasing accusations. Your prayer time should be used to pray for issues that are important. Let the Lord fight for you. Moses never once put away his wife and family because of his relative's opinions. These were not the only people he had to deal with. The sons of Korah also rose up against Moses. What he did under these circumstances was go up to the mountaintop during these times and get instructions from God. Go up while others are pulling you down. It may not be with their physical hands, and frankly, they are too much of a coward to do this. It will be with words, silence, and manipulation. Altitude is what planes and helicopters need to fly. When they reach a certain peak, objects become smaller; noise is drowned out; and you are surrounded by clouds. We, too, have been invited to run to a rock that is higher than us. We are surrounded by a great cloud of witnesses who are martyrs.

Christ has freely given us all things pertaining to life and godliness. Moses went to the pharaoh, and each time, his heart got harder. Remember the Lord hardened his heart. I asked the question why would the Lord do this? Yet he sent Moses to deliver the children of Israel. There will be no blessings without a battle. The Bible talks of great victories, but battles were fought to win them. The journey was from the first church, which was an old bar with a capacity fifty seats. Our newest facility holds a capacity of one hundred ten seats. None of these locations were not birthed without a fight. God never puts you in a battle without giving all the weapons you need to win. "For the weapons of our warfare are not carnal but mighty in God for pulling down strongholds" (2 Cor. 10:4).

Each time Moses went to the pharaoh, he refused him; the nation was stuck. He received an answer the people were going to be set free only after the last plague. Moses was ready to act. No more excuses about his inadequacies. We can all be honest; there are assignments when we question ourselves. Are you sure you want me to do this? In the most difficult times on the journey, we, too, have struck the rock instead of speaking to it out of frustration. Good news: These are the times when God is closest to us. He created us and he knows we are fallible. Stay focused during these times and take the high road to victory.

Your exodus is at hand, "Acknowledge him in all your ways and He will direct your path."(Prov.3:5) Confusion only comes when we begin to veer away from the destination. It is in those times that we stop, inquire of the Lord, and wait for His instruction before we move. Waiting will save you from wanting in the end. It's not uncommon for me to stop in the middle of a project and ask for redirection. This is the moment where many people go astray. You see, this is where many freedom is a beautiful thing when it is handled correctly.

They begin to say, "Okay, I've got this, God, you can go ahead." We don't realize that God never takes his eyes off us. The enemy is seeking whom he may devour; there's nothing wrong with changing your mind. It doesn't mean you are double-minded either. When a person is unsure and have taken the time to refocus, it allows the Lord to enlighten the eyes of your understanding. It gives you fresh vision, and you are added to, rather than depleted. Moses rewrote the Ten Commandments after coming down from the mountain and finding the Israelites making a golden calf. Moses broke the first commandment because of this. God will rewrite some things in our lives. It would be better and a blessing for you.

NO PARKING

*P*arking meters give you a limited time for parking according to the time you purchased. When God provides a way out for you, don't be at a standstill. Keep it moving at the pace in the race, which is set for you. It's hard to shoot down a moving target. Anyone who is doing anything significant for the kingdom of God is a threat to the devil. You cannot allow fear to paralyze you. The Israelites were aware of the enemies that occupied their land, and they were going to have to fight to conquer it. The instructions given to them was to pack light and get ready to leave. They were never told in detail what lay ahead in the wilderness.

God does not always give us details because he doesn't want us to derail. Do not forget to carry the bones of Joseph were the instructions given to the Israelites as they journeyed to the freedom. It reminded them of the seven years of plenty during the famine. I like to look at old photos and see where the Lord brought me from. My new photos revealed to me where he was leading me to. Onward, Christian soldiers, we shall not go out empty. I know that this book may transition back and forth about exodus, the reason being is because there are important factors you must know in every wilderness situation. They were wandering for some time in the wilderness, but God knew eventually they would reach their destination.

Previously I told of my departure from full-time employment. I was stripped of two weeks' vacation and other benefits afforded to me because of the haste in my resignation. This left me with only a paycheck and some resources from the former company who owned us. I believe in my twenty-one-year tenure, the company changed on us four times. If you make a wholehearted decision to follow, God will your finance trip if He sent you on the journey. In the former chapters, I mentioned the day I resigned, my vehicle broke down. I had a mortgage and a child in college. <u>These are the times in my life that I questioned God.</u> Faith doesn't wait for the perfect time it presents itself at the right time. All that's required of us is to step out. It's the same risk that Peter took when he walked on water. He will raise up somebody somewhere to use their power and ability to bless you. I was able get my auto repair and pay my mortgage in full. This allowed me to start up the ministry by faith until I could build the congregation. I was not getting a salary for the first six years of the ministry. My spouse had been employed for forty-eight years, so he was the sole support for our household.

God will do us just like He did the Israelites when they needed water or food. They cried to God, and He provided for them. I felt like Ruth gleaning in the fields of Boaz. God was dropping handfuls down for me in these times. God teaches us to be faithful in the few, and he will make you ruler over many. My son received a job as an intern with an engineering firm. He had his own finances for room and board at the home of an engineer. It was fully furnished with all the amenities. God has proven to me that my life has already been planned out. He is not like man that He should lie. If He said it, He would make it good; if He spoke, he will bring it to pass. He is a good Father; that's who He is, and I am loved by Him.

Don't get stuck in the mud of life with a routine where everyone does the same thing expecting different results. If it hasn't produced fruit by now, that's a sure sign that you need a new gardening technique. The Israelites left Egypt's hard labor of brickmaking, which requires a person to use more than mortar and mud. They often referred to going back because their mentality was stuck in the mud. This type of mindset can sabotage your future. Yet many unknowingly are stuck. Don't keep your vision merely a vision board, and don't allow the legs of your faith to be amputated. Pigs will roll in the mud; it's their way of cooling off. If you put ribbons around their neck, and if they are anywhere in proximity of a mudhole, they will be headed for it. How long they have been there will determine what you will need to pull them out.

John 8:32 says, "And you shall know the truth and the truth shall make you free." You can only walk in the level of freedom from the truth you know. The longer you stay in the mud, it begins to harden. If it gets to the brick stage, then you'll be forced to get a hammer and bust it into pieces. We are God's battle-ax. We are weapons of war. With us He will break nations into pieces. We are the change agent He wants to see in the world. I love to read the Word and other books; I believe the Word is active and alive, sharper than any two-edged sword. The generation we call the millennials don't just want to hear God; they want to see a demonstration of power. Paul knew words alone wouldn't convinced the people. Jesus knew that signs and wonders were the key to convince people that He was the Messiah. Moses was equipped by God to use what was in his hand, a staff he threw on the ground and it turned into a serpent. He picked it up and it returned to a staff. Moses parted the Red Sea for the children of Israel to cross over with this same staff. Pharaoh and the children Israel saw that God was with him. God had already equipped Moses with what he needed.

STAY IN THE RACE

We get so concerned with the outcome that we don't come out of the holding block and run the race that is set before us. If you are reading this, I plead with you get out of the mud and leave the place of complacency. The gun has gone off; did you hear it? Get going before you fall behind in the race. The children of Israel were instructed to carry the bones of Joseph with them into the promised land. A skeleton is a reminder that once, this person lived and breathed on this earth just like you. In life you will have successes and great events happen to you. It has been an influential person God sent on assignment in your life to help you out. When a person is sent by God, you will know it. Divine connection between the two of you. They will bring addition into your life. Jonathan and David came to mind when I think of this kind of relationship. The Bible says their souls were knitted together. God gave me a Jonathan at the at the most critical time of my ministry. It's not at the finish line where you need the cheers; it's at the start when you see nothing, It's at the halfway mark when you are out of wind and you want to throw your hands up and quit. These people may look nothing like you pictured they would be, People who would have never taken any interest in you. Their presence often come with presents. These are presents of knowledge, wisdom, power, influence, connections, and wealth. Aaron was there for Moses to speak; Jethro was there for him for advice, and his wife was there to provide a family atmosphere for him. Don't forget people who stood with you in the beginning stages, as well as the people who finished with you. An important factor in staying out of the wilderness is loyalty to those who decided to stay. There's a key for every door that seems to have no exit. Peter had the keys to unlock and lock. He had direct access to the throne room.

You also have the same privileges to bind and loose. People stay in place and a position entirely too long because they have keys but they won't use them. The keys won't fit, or the other reason could be that they've lost their keys. Debt is a wilderness many find themselves in because they won't be content with what they have. Seek debt counseling, preferably Christian debt counseling because they would honor tithing as a part of your budget. God never intended for us to ignore or escape obligations to lenders. The Word warns us about the debtor being a slave to the lender.

How long do you want to be a slave? Twelve months interest free or seventy-two months? Paying extra will cut down the interest and lower your contract over a certain period. See yourself paying ninety days same as cash or paying cash for your purchases. Add up your debt and draw up a plan and stick to the plan. I literally had to lock away my credit cards for a year in order to pay off a recent furniture purchase in a year. I can remember living in a cycle of card debt credit, card cash advances, and personal loans. I had to file bankruptcy twenty years ago only to repeat the same cycle over again. Debt will make you blame tithing for your financial shortage. The problem most people have is managing the 90 percent you have left. Purchasing value meals for a week may not be a value. Shopping from a clearance rack is no different than having the dress that's on the mannequin. You make the outfit no matter what the cost. Get creative and move things around. Switch them up. Sometimes I wear five different shirts with one pair of pants or a skirt. Get your four basic shoe colors. I purchase hose in bulk quantity so every week you're not paying for a pair. Choosing gel polish over regular will result in a longer lasting effect. I can see why people are going natural with their hair. Back to the basics is really the best key to use for a financial wilderness. Any keys of wisdom I can pass on to the next generation is just like giving them wealth. Educate your church, children, and anyone who will listen. I had a young man pour about thirty years of financial wisdom into my life in two hours. His advice was so solid it made you perk up and listen to him. Cliques is another type wilderness I had to walk out of. This will rob a person of their individuality and vitality. You begin to conform to the ways of who you associate the most with. Be a people person, but being yourself is key. You should never be the smartest person in your circle, because then who will you glean and grow from? I have found that relationships with people older than me has saved me from a lot of traps in life. Relationships with knowledgeable people have given me insight of things I would never have known. Networking with others works in implementing vision. No one person knows it all.

Settlers will do what their name says: they will always settle. It can be with a job, man, woman, lifestyle, or ministry. People can become too predictable and begin to live life in cycles. You can just about pinpoint what they would do in every situation. Ministries who never allow the spirit of the Lord to dictate the service never experience all of God's glory. Jericho had a similar problem. It was straightly shut up and no could get out and no one could get in. Maybe you have been hurt so deeply that you try and protect yourself. Allow God to heal you so that you can trust and love again. Do not allow your past hurt to hinder you bright future. I had to learn to love people on purpose by intentionally going above and beyond to make things better for someone and doing thoughtful deeds after studying that person and evaluating what makes them happy.

Loving without a purpose robs you and the recipient of the expected end. God loves us with the purpose. He sent his Son to die for our sins, and this freed us from being a slave to sin. I recall a story shared with me by a friend when she visited a young lady with sores all over her body. Her odor was not as pleasant to the smell. She began to pray for this young lady she recalled hearing these words, "Can you love her back to life." Love will bring the most lifeless situation back from the dead. Many divorces would not have happened if love was rekindled. We would destroy all the records of wrong that has been compiled over the years against someone. Jesus knew it would take a special love for mankind. He so loved us that anytime the enemy wants to bring up our past mistakes, your past does not shock Jesus. Everything hinges on love—the gifts, the miracles, and salvation. We need God in order to love properly. When it's done right, you will love that person back to life. Forgiveness is another key to unlock one from the wilderness. God will put you in a position where you can't continue to hold that person hostage. You will decide to let them go free. It's like having the position of a juror to decide the fate of an individual. This will help you look at their present situation and allow God's compassion to fall on you. Turn them over to God. Walk on in the peace that passes all understanding. This is when your heart and mind will feel a release from all the bondage that held you down. There are times when you can't see who you hold hostage. Intentionally things are done to trigger an address issues of the heart. Wilderness times expose the good and the bad in all of us. We may find ourselves like Peter, who asked, "Lord how often do I forgive my brother?" Jesus answered, "Seventy times seven." The same offense could happen for years. If you continue to respond the same way, you will get the same results.

Extend forgiveness. Release them and leave them in the wilderness. There are people who will not want to follow you out. Remember when the prison door opens, the prisoners will be afraid and don't immediately come out. Right connections are a vital key to favor. Moses being drawn from the water caused him to be related to the pharaoh. Moses refused to be called the son of pharaoh but be identified with his people, when he approached him with the ultimatum to let God's people go. Moses knew God caused him to lead a nation to freedom. Connections are good if they are divine and both parties will jointly benefit from it. When we put too much emphasis on an individual for a success, that is unwise. Years ago, I had started the manuscript for this book, and I told people. I even met others who were writing as well, only to be in competition and not have connection.

Can two walk together except they be agreed? (Amos 3:3 KJV). It is ok to disagree and not be disagreeable to change. Difference of opinions can give you a different perspective. Moses and Aaron could accomplish much together because they both knew the same person intimately, which was God. Joshua and Caleb could lead the people together because they believe that they were well able to take the land. Ruth and Naomi survived the famine because they returned to Bethlehem. The door He shuts, no man can open. We will find ourselves in these times frustrated and trying to pry it open. The ten virgins learned this lesson well when the bridegroom came, only those who were ready went in with him. How much time is wasted when preparation should have been taking place. God will never send you anywhere you are not prepared for. God is not in the business of seeing his children fall or fail. It's our own doing when we are not prepared for an open door. Moses stayed on the backside of the desert for more than killing the Egyptian; that was a time for preparation. It was there he had the burning bush encounter and received instructions for the exodus of the children of Israel. God is not afraid of crowded rooms, but He does his best to work behind closed doors. This also gave Moses a chance to close the door on the guilt of killing the Egyptian. I have found that if you close the door on some places, people, position, and properties, then you can see clearly in view what God has opened for you. Every good builder clears the land before putting something on it.

Clear the land and rise and build. In the words of the Apostle Paul, "Brethren I count not myself to have apprehended but this one thing I do forgetting those things which are behind and reaching forth unto those things which are before" (Phil. 3:13). Decide what is beneficial, not every function requires your attendance. Another nugget for life is to never allow anyone's presence to take precedence over you. Ready yourself for a position in Christ rather than running after a position you may not be ready for. God is still giving his people territory, so let him pick the property. I remember vividly when I desired a home, every day I would ride around in different cities and pray and believe God for my home. One day, in prayer, He spoke to me, "Stop looking. It's not built yet." He showed me what type and color to look for—red brick with white poles. I stopped looking for a season, then I pursued my search again in my hometown. There was a new construction going up, so I went by this house and saw the white poles. I happily went up and asked what color would the house be. The builder said he wasn't sure. Construction continued until they applied the stucco brick, which was the color red. I knew this was the house. I loaded up my kids. We drove by and I asked the builder whom I should contact about the house. He said that the house was already sold to someone. All I had was a word, but that's all I needed. I continued my same devotion and prayer time at six. The family knew that this was an uninterrupted time and not to disturb me. God longs to have fellowship with us, therefore he created mankind.

One afternoon my attention was drawn to Hebrews 11. I read the whole chapter by faith. This one and that one received the promise but not all. I said, "That won't be me, Lord, you're going to give us a house." You would have thought that living in a home for only $200 monthly rent with a fireplace, I would have been content. The house was cold, and I had to use the assistance of an oven to heat it. I had to secure the door entrances because at one point, a poisonous snake crawled into my daughters' room. It was in this house that I was called to ministry at the ironing board. I gave birth to our son, who brought peace, joy, and awareness to our family. I remember like yesterday because of daylight savings, it was dark after my time of prayer. Because of my persistence I left my name and number with the people who lived at the back of that house. The owners of the house resided in my present neighborhood.

My phone rang, and the voice on the other end said, "Are you still interested in the house?"

I exclaimed, "Yes."

"I am the former client's agent. They had a change of plans and are not going to buy it."

Even if someone occupied the land, no worries, God will give it to you if it's yours. People were living in the promised land, which belongs to the Israelites. God drove some of them out. Israel had to fight. They got their territory. When you come to a place of faith in your life where you see the promise, watch your fellowship. It does matter in this season who you connect with. This is not friendship; it is fellowship. God chooses the people who will be strategic in your progress. God doesn't allow covetous, jealous, or envious people to go far; they will drop off. Judas went so far with Jesus, but He couldn't go to the destination. The entire tribe of Israel didn't make it to the promised land. This will allow you to keep them at the table because this may be as far as the Lord allows them to go. These people may never share your stage. Moses taught me a valuable lesson about leadership: never allow those you are leading to cause you to abort your destiny with their distractions. He only allowed the distractions of the people to abort his destination.

Twelve spies were sent out, but all didn't see the same thing. If they can't see your vision, they will never partake of the fruit. God did not make you a grasshopper. The people saw the land, but the giants occupied it, and they saw themselves as grasshoppers because of the size of the Anakites. Get a new view of the new you. The person created in Christ Jesus for good works. Image to some people is everything. I have spent thousands to keep up with the latest fads and hairstyle. All this is what Solomon said is vanity. The most important thing a believer can do is work on the upkeep of their spiritual house. Keep it built up in your most holy faith, singing songs and speaking melodies to yourself. The only way to keep your sanity is to keep a song in your heart. Moses had a song. He said firsthand how he saw the Lord deliver them from the horse and the rider. I'm not being boastful, but I got to brag on my God, and I have not lost many battles. I've learned not to go to battle without him. He lets me know you won't need to fight in this battle. There are times when he says don't fight in this battle; hold your peace in this battle; don't say a word. It appeared as if there was no way out for the children of Israel, so it may appear that there is no way out for you. This is your exodus. Follow Him, and He will lead you out of any situation every time. Forward is a gear you want to stay in if you are planning on doing anything significant in life. A car doesn't even move until you put it in gear and start it up. People waste more time procrastinating than starting. A dream is still in a holding pattern until it started up like a car. It's important that we keep a full tank of faith.

Doing regular maintenance on our souls as we progress forward is vital at the beginning stage of vision. The roadblocks are sent to put you in park. I was pulled over for speeding, and the officer asked for my license and registration. I had the license but not the registration. If he didn't have the technology to research the registration, they wouldn't know who the car belonged to. Make sure you slow down as you move forward, and let the world know you belong to God. I ran under a yellow light. There were cameras in the traffic light. It took a picture of my tag and I was issued a citation. People are always watching you, and it's important that you be a light in this dark world. God has called all of us to the Great Commission. Have you yielded to him? Are you in neutral and halt between two opinions? Move forward and proceed with caution. Driving forward requires your visual to be intact. The side mirrors now are designed to light up when cars are very close to you so you won't crossover into another's lane. We need a mechanism in our hearts to show us we have unknowingly crossed over in someone's lane. It can happen so quickly and innocently. Taking on assignments that you are not graced to do.

You also have a rearview mirror which role is to give you a glance of what's behind. Rearview mirrors help us see the traffic behind us. We cannot stay focused on what is behind us too long; it's only meant for you to glance. Look forward and see how much closer you are to your destination. It was only when the children of Israel looked back that they saw all the chariots and horsemen behind them. This made them afraid. It may have filled them with anxiety about what lies ahead. You can have a wreck looking in your rearview mirror too long. There are many destinies lying on heap piles in junkyards because they refused to look ahead and move forward. Set your sights on the future and not your past.

It's been proven you can get water out of the rock. Jesus told Peter because of the revelation he had of who he was, it really made Peter who he was, rock-solid in faith. Water quenches the thirst, washes something clean, and causes things to grow. The Word of God says He came to give us the living water. We are not to keep it to ourselves but to share it with the thirsty. Moses had everything was needed to lead. Find out what you're working with and utilize it to bring change. Today more than ever, we need to be rock-solid in our belief in God. There are so many mirages that the enemy is throwing, and Christians are taking the bait. If you are wandering in the desert long enough, you will see a mirage of water, whether a lake spring or just a cup. It looks so real until you reach for it only to find out it was a mirage. A three-day journey turned into a forty-day one only because their faith in God and in the leadership, God ordained for them was not rock-solid.

God chooses shepherds after his own heart. The Father knows what's best for you. There is a Red Sea in front of us. What exactly can you do when there is a roadblock in your destiny path? Get a different viewpoint. That's when God will give you a strategy. Those in the back of the line couldn't see what was ahead of them. Moses led a nation of people, not a tribe. Those in the back of the line saw the chariots in hot pursuit behind them. That's when God will speak and act on your behalf. These Egyptians you see today, you should see no more. It's what's in front of you that would take care of what's behind you. God wants to drown out all the doubt and fear that keeps us from our destiny. He said He would open a door that no man can close. He will open a highway up in a sea and close it up right in the nick of time. I've seen God firsthand bring me through many things and shut the door on any aftermath that would attempt to come after me. The rider and the horsemen have no control over you. Believe God is in control of your journey through life.

There is another level of trusting God we have never tapped into. Crossover. He's already on the other side waiting you. You will see in detail the course of events that led me out of the wilderness of uncertainty, insecurity, and insanity. You will not always know what to do in every situation. There will be times when your thoughts would be clouded. You will also be fearful of taking risks and trusting people. Sometimes you can't distinguish a friend from foe. Your discernment is not activated to locate the smallest error. There are mind battles like you would not believe. You long for quiet times just to get peace of mind from constantly thinking. You question yourself, Am I losing it? Friends and family may not always tell you they think that you are a little extra. This may seem abnormal, but it is reality; it is happening to many people whom Satan is losing his grip on. Pharaoh didn't want to let go, and neither does Satan. Stay in close fellowship through prayer and fasting. It will loosen every band that tries to hold you. He will free you from oppression of anything and anyone who would get in the path of you leaving. I had to leave before I left, but that's another chapter. Pressure can do one or two things in a person's life. Let it press you down, or you will press on. Too much is given, much is required implies that God wouldn't give what we can't handle.

Some people are multitaskers; others can do one assignment. Demands from schedules, people, and personal challenges of your own can apply this pressure. It requires a deadline that cannot be ignored. These are the times when you prioritize your time and spend it well. Determination has little time for distraction. I will wait for his strength in times like these. God told Gideon go in the strength that you have. It was with this amount of strength Gideon would need to defeat the Midianites. Operating in His strength gives you a grace to do the task ahead without dread. If you cannot do something without complaining or murmuring the entire time, you should wait and rest until you can give it your all. Doing things in the spirit of excellency, this sets one individual apart from another and makes a lasting impact on the recipient. Do not allow the spirit of jealousy to arise when another person is preferred instead of you. Take under consideration all the effort that was done by that individual. God gave us all He had when He gave us His Son. Give Him your all when He puts responsibilities in your hands. On it!

A premature exodus happens when a leader stops leading. Moses began to allow the pressure when he let other people frustrate him so much that he hit the rock instead of speaking to it. This cost him the promised land. He saw it but never entered it. Don't allow all your labor to be in vain. Remember that were twelve spies sent out. Only two came back with a good report. Moses broke commandments because while in his absence, the people built a golden calf. Leading cannot proceed without loving, then learning. God will give you the love for the people you are called to. You must not assume they know everything. You as a leader will not know everything. This only makes a better people easier to lead. Few leaders want to disciple people because it takes time, patience, and practice. You may have to reiterate something multiple times before they grasp it. Jesus used most of his three years of ministry teaching his disciples. He used parables as comparing spiritual things with natural. Moses had the wisdom to duplicate himself through Joshua. The mark of a good leader is not in numbers, but it is there in anyone in the number that leader can reduplicated themselves by training and impartation.

How you handle hard times will determine how you handle blessings. These are the times that personal sacrifices are made and integrity is built upon. God will see if we are stewards over small things before, he allows us to be rulers over much. Keep three bedrooms clean before you ask for six bedrooms. Dry-clean the outfit from Macy's, then you would take care of the one from Bloomingdale's. Is that Ford washed and vacuumed weekly and the maintenance up-to-date? This will determine how well you will take care of Jaguar you are praying for. Ministry takes maintenance; you become a keeper of God's resources, His people, church, grounds, and finances.

Early stages of ministry are times you need to operate in divine wisdom. Staying in faith is crucial part of success or failure. Suppose your congregation is small, will you have the faith to operate as if it were large? Can God ask you to put the best in His church? I remember having two church lawns that needed servicing. I hired a lawn service because I wanted to start like I wanted to finish. If you start with the two-member congregation, get the tithe envelopes, get the accounting program uploaded, and order the chairs. Hard times will cause miracles to happen. Keep a positive attitude in this season. It can determine your outcome. Remember Ruth appreciated the handfuls until she owned the house. Your faith will finance it. Have you ever planned to do something great and the money wasn't there? Faith will finance dreams and visions.

Nehemiah only had a sad countenance, and the king noticed it. This prompted him to ask him what was wrong. Nehemiah told the king of the condition of his city and how he desired to rebuild. The king sent letters to all his connections, and Nehemiah got the materials he needed for reconstruction. Giving someone your last may exhaust all your resources. Follow your heart; you will not regret it. I had nothing but my faith on November 2015. The current location of the church I leased up was up for auction. I had carpet installed, chairs placed, and decorated it as if it belongs to us. Faith will always have you act as if it's already done. Abraham told his servants, "Me and the lad will be back." The lad saw the wood and built the fire, but where was the sacrifice? The Lord will provide.

When the bidding started, I sat quietly, and the owner said, "You're not going to bid?" I finally bid at $10,000 and didn't have $10. I knew someone who had all the money I needed, his name is Jesus. The bidding got higher; I remained silent but calm. The final bid was $64,000. The owners wanted 125,000, so they divided the parcels of land between two parties. I went back inside the church.

The church administrator said, "Pastor, what are we going to do?"

I replied, "God is not through yet!"

The new property owner came in, looked around, and said, "You have done an excellent job with this building. I don't want your church. I'm going to have some papers drawn up and sell it back to you with interest."

I said, "Thank you!"

I had about twenty members at time, and I had awfully bad credit. I remember seeing the joy on the administrator's face when this was said it was not over until God said it was over. There have been many situations where I've seen the hand of God. I expect every time I'm in the heat of the battle to win. My trust is in the Lord, and He won't fail. When we as a believer begin to rely on God at that level, we will see Red Seas parted, burning bushes, and Egyptian enemies. Today we should see no more. Your viewpoint can point you right in the right or wrong direction. I chose to see God in every attribute His Word describes Him. The administrator had a dream of a group of Caucasian men in white shirts and blue jeans present at the auction. Suddenly, they turned into angels with wings. There were men dressed exactly like she saw it. The earthly angel God used was dressed exactly as she saw it. He stepped up, and he bought the property.

A wise man once told me, "God is raising up someone some-where to use their power and ability to bless you." On December 2015, the church was my greatest Christmas present. On December 2019, a thirty-year mortgage was completed in five years with fifty members. He's a miracle worker! Aaron did not mind assisting his brother, Moses and fulfilling the role as high priest. He was an important part of the spiritual leadership role in the lives of the Israelites. Moses led them out of Egypt because they couldn't freely worship. Knowing your role in the body is a very important piece of fulfilling the assignment that is given to you. All can't be the eye, hand, or foot. You can't say you don't need that one. When any part of someone's natural body is a missing limb, we can say that person is disfigured. The body of Christ has become disfigured when all the parts are not functioning in the significant roles together. Potential always points to your strengths. Saul hated David because of his anointing. David's strengths outweigh his weaknesses because he was a man after God's own heart. Many times people don't like you, but they like what you can do. David's music soothed Saul's troubled spirit. When the anointing leaves a person, you better leave or you will become a target for their spear. They won't literally throw spears; they will hurl insults and seek to take your life.

People who are dead in their trespasses will envy your life. They will seek to take your life; go away until it's your time to reign. Due diligence is a key factor in moving a vision. Most people rejoice at the finished product. The careful and persistent work or effort an individual invests in accomplishing the goal is what counts. Day after day, the Israelites had to keep walking. I'm sure they were inclined to complain because they hadn't seen a glimpse of their destination. It's like putting together a puzzle: the box top shows you the result, but it will not look like the picture that is shown unless the right pieces are put into place.

Many times, we stop being persistent when we face setbacks, criticisms, or when everything we need is not available. Times like these should cause us to get a bulldog tenacity and not kitten profile. God needs someone who will walk through the adversity and turn it into an adventure. Ninety percent of people turn around before they reach their destination. Life is choice driven and the choices we make decides the life we live. That's very powerful because we tend to want to blame others for how things turned out. I was told when you point a finger, there's always one pointed back at you. Well, we are no different than the Israelites when it comes to the wilderness times in our life. We say audibly an internally, "Why did you bring us out here into the wilderness to die?"

I remember like yesterday getting the keys to our new location for the church. The church was remembered for having flooded during the hurricane. The interesting thing was that the water only could come up to three feet around the perimeter of the church. I want you to know sometimes you're promised land is not pretty. You must cultivate the land yourself. The Israelites had to process and build their own houses. God can do it all, but I believe we would have no muscles in our faith if He did that. He did that for Adam and Eve; Adam was to name everything and fellowship with God. Disobedience will destroy everything God has given to you if you fall prey to the enemy. Failure to fellowship with God would cause you to be without the very guidance you need. I was given the promise that it was up to me to make it a palace. I was working a full-time job as a director, so every morning, about 4:00 a.m., I will go down and paint a wall. I was so proud of that little step of progress. My administrator would help me when she could. Together we saw the pieces of the puzzle come together. I looked at the lighting, and it seemed to be intact. I came home and the ceiling fans kept staying in my thoughts. I purchased new ones and proceeded to hang them with the assistance of another pastor. I got to the last fan, and it was only held up by only one bolt and would have eventually fell and hurt a parishioner.

God gave Solomon the plans for the temple; He's a master architect. The next phase was the flooring. I used the same company that I did for the former church. He is a fellow Christian, so he took the details of the job seriously. Before any carpeting could be installed, the stage needs to be extended a few feet. The owner purchased the lumber and had it put on the stage at no extra charge. How awesome is that! The sound was the next installation, so Carlton Music and Guitar Center were the two vendors I used. The two gentlemen who installed the speakers were believers and gave me suggestions to buy quality now and not have to purchase again later. God gave me favor with the owner of one of the music stores. He came to Fort Meade and personally tweaked the microphones for us. I still use the same microphones eleven years later. I started with very little money, but God gave me favor with vendors, electricians, construction companies, and plumbers. I was able to pay monthly installments. God gave me favor with these vendors and over-time we built a trust factor.

Out with the old pews and in with the new furniture, the sanctuary holds about one hundred ten chairs. I had fifty chairs already from the old sanctuary. I had a lot of supporters from my job. I printed out a donation letter for the chairs for the sanctuary. Every chair was purchased that I asked for. All sixty chairs were purchased. The picture may not look like the promise until you are persistent in the process. Any individual who has accomplished anything great has paid a price. Jesus sacrificed his life, so we could live. Something worth having is worth the sacrifice. Sweat equity is all that Habitat of Humanity ask of an individual to obtain their first home. You may say you have never built anything before, but the very thought of ownership would give you the desire to drive a nail in some wood. The signup sheet gets multiple volunteers on it because of you setting a standard. Sacrifice becomes easier when one can see the benefits. Become the sacrifice you want others to be. I have seen in my years as a believer the thing asked of others are not carried out by the team leader themselves.

The Bible ask us to be first partakers. We always want to associate with the fruit only. What about the labor, tilling the ground, sowing the seed, turning the soil, and watering it on a consistent basis? Be a part of the solution and not the problem. Team up and don't tear down. I don't want anything that hasn't cost me something but my salvation. It keeps my faith fresh and the fight ongoing. We have no time to waste. Time is like money spent wisely, and it will buy you what you need. The Israelites were known for their ability to give birth. I believe this is one of the most powerful tools God equipped us with as women. The pain is no longer remembered after the joy of seeing your baby. It is no different with your vision. You are going to experience pain, disappointment and discomfort; enjoy all those different stages. Remember God will always give you a midwife. The midwife was instructed to kill every male child and keep the girls. Satan is trying to keep us from giving birth, but we have a midwife who is armed and ready to assist in delivery. He won't allow your dream to be aborted. We also play a key role, just like carrying a child. We must take care of ourselves; get the proper rest and things we need to produce a healthy vision. All visions are not healthy if it is prematurely launched before time. It will be a stillborn vision if it was not launched in time. It will be dead, meaning it was never launched. All types of birth come with pain, and you still must push.

Society has us wanting things quick fast and in a hurry. A mother carries a baby for thirty-six weeks to consider it full term. Visions maybe carried thirty-six years, but it does not mean that one day your water will not break, and you will give birth. God will order a sonogram in the process to give you hope of what is to come. Abraham believed in hope against all hope and obtained the promise. Today I want to encourage someone and let you know you shall prevail. I remember the movie *Rambo*. After an explosive fight, when the smoke cleared, out walks Rambo the star of the show. He was unharmed, maybe a few scratches, but everything was still intact. We may go through the storms in life and the odds may be slim chances of survival, but you will prevail. This is a word I was given a few years back when I made a major decision to move the church in a new direction, same location but new focus. When the Bible says put your trust in no man, it literally means don't rely so much on others' opinions. It distorts your vision. God created us to come to Him and worship Him. I believe because we can't physically touch or see God, we desire to have someone or something that's tangible. I have not regretted the decision I made on behalf of the church. We are continuing to go forward. Those are days I feel inadequate for the role. Those are the days I say in times when I'm afraid I will trust in thee. He had never failed me yet.

This is the trouble Moses had with the Israelites. They wanted to hear the instructions from God, not Moses. They began to complain about this and wanted to hear from God themselves. The time came for this to occur, and when it happened, they were afraid. One instance, Moses was in a battle on their behalf, and his arms got tired. Aaron and Hur held up Moses's arms and Israel prevailed. *Pursue* is another word you must remember; go after the promise.

I have seen people hope and pray for years without manifestation, and their excuse was "I'm just waiting for God." He is waiting for us. God will instruct us to wait, but it's after you have done all humanly possible that can be done. People don't like being told no! This is the reason marking time is better for them. It is a military action where soldiers pick their feet up and down but never move forward. It looks like movement without motion. Pursuit takes you to unfamiliar places, people, and things. We don't like to admit that religion has followed us home. Religion is when people turn serving into a routine. Routine ruins the very essence of purpose. Purpose is what fuels pursuit. Unless you have this in your life, you literally are at a standstill. Without this important ingredient burning within Moses, the children of Israel would have died in the wilderness. Moses was in pursuit of the promise given to him by God.

In the movie *Pursuit of Happiness*, Will Smith tried multiple times to get a medical invention off the ground. He finds himself homeless with a child to raise. Despite the circumstances, his pursuit gave him determination that was needed. Moses crossed the Red Sea, and Will mastered his invention. I'm writing this book because of my pursuit for the promise. Persistence is that bulldog tenacity that keeps one moving. Bite into your vision and get your teeth in it and lock down. Have you ever seen someone trying to get a dog to lose his grip on something? They literally must drag the dog an all that is in its mouth. This is the same way it should be with vision; You and your vision should be a package deal. Tough times have a tough time with a persistent person. Parking is not an option with these type people; they are your late-night hawks and early risers. They have five-to-ten-year goals, constantly marking short-term goals off their vision board. Visionaries are not all in corporate America. They are ordinary people with the drive to accomplish something. Anyone looking to accomplish something worthwhile, you want them as a part of your team. I call them thinkers because they have already thought through tomorrow and possibly next week. No one is born a leader. There are certain quality traits that will set you above the norm. People want achievers all their talents cannot be articulated on a resume. It must be given a task and observed overtime. Anyone who has ever been promoted possesses this quality. Moses handed over the reins to Joshua, and he got the job done. I get to make memories now with my life. One day I may be able to show my grandchildren and the next generation. I really live, and I see the scriptures come alive in my life. I have time to enjoy my family and take care of the church properly. I can spend hours in the presence of the Lord uninterrupted.

I recently had my mom came to live with us, which was another part of my inner healing from my childhood. I was raised by my grandmother, but my mother supported us and visited often. This isn't the same as having your parents in the home. She had a stroke that left her somewhat incapacitated, but little did we know all things work together for the good. This is when a generational curse of unnecessary debt was broken off our family line. God has a way of answering us of prayers that we pray for an exodus whether from dead weight or unhealthy relationship that may take some time to understand. My experience of being in the rehabilitation environment helped me to continue exercising with my mom to strengthen her muscles. We formed a budget that eliminated a lot of debt. I was able to see my mother not only recover from her illness, but her finances were healed as well. "And Moses said to the people, "Don't be afraid to stand still and see the salvation of the Lord, which he will show you today; For the Egyptians whom you have seen today ye shall see them again no more forever. The Lord shall fight for you and ye shall hold your peace (Exodus 14:13,14 KJV).

A true leader always trains a successor, but normally, it's one person. I had trained about five people who could do my job without fail. Sickness knocked one of them out of the lineup. You can only lead as good as you follow—a lesson to be learned by anyone aspiring to lead. They hired a person for the position and the elevation went straight to their head, I was aware then that the tenure in the position wouldn't be long. Respect is earned overtime and so is trust. The totality and reality of a thing hits you overtime. You can never remain where you are not ready for. It's not always as easy as it appears. What looks appealing to your eyes, you may need to look a little further into it.

Judas hung himself. Misaligned ambition will cause you to hang yourself. If you aspire to advance, never undermine anyone to get there. Whatever you did to get it, you will have to continue to keep it. A stubborn person is likened to a mule. Mules *hee* and *haw* and will kick you. This is the reaction of a stubborn person. They will buck against just about everything you do. Since the will is involved, they are determined that they will not budge. No matter how much you promote unity, they will fight against it. Rebellion is as the sin of witchcraft Stubbornness is another form of rebellion. They may remain but will fight the vision silently. Though they may even make it through the wilderness with you, they have their own agenda in mind all the time. When you arrive to your destiny, the stubborn person would say, "Is this it? I thought everything would be already set up" We worked hard in Egypt; now we have become Moses's slaves." You see, a person of this mindset does not like following leadership. God doesn't mind these people coming alone; you shouldn't let them upset you either. There needs to be an audience when signs and wonders are manifested. This is a good audience to have God perform for. He convinced the pharaoh to do was needed. Many people wring their hands and worry over the necessities of life. I have found that if you do what's needed, it would be the right decision.

Mary and Martha were waiting for Jesus to arrive. Martha was busy getting things prepared. Mary must have not been doing the portion of the workload Martha felt was fair. Martha was still working but probably murmuring under her breath. This is no different than a person who would volunteer and do something in the church and complain because others may not quickly even jump on the bandwagon. They should not allow this to affect the decision they made, but usually they do. Martha begins to tell him of all the all the current events. Jesus asked her why she was bothered by so many things. He said Mary has chosen the good part. Mary was sitting at his feet and worshiping him. Sitting at his feet was exactly what Moses did when he went up and had the burning bush experience. Jesus often did this apart for those disciples.

I rise sometimes 2:00 a.m. or 4:00 a.m. to spend time with the Lord before my busy day starts. All through the day, I stop and take little intervals and thank God. He came to raise Lazarus from the grave. Resurrection power comes from the Lord. You can stand in awe at his mighty works because you chose the best part.

INTERRUPTIONS

*A*ll interruptions are not to get you off track, but on the contrary, you could find a sweet release in the interruption if it's set up by God. The promised land was not a straight shot. Stay focused, even with interruptions by going back to the disciplines you have put in place for your life. Rest is especially important when God is bringing you into your promise land. I can't see it right then until my pen hits the page.

Young love is so beautiful and innocent. It reminds me of when I first gave my heart to the Lord. Over the years, my love for the Lord has gotten more intense. He truly is the lover of my soul. Fellowship helps me with leadership. I know somewhat how Adam must have felt when he was taken out of Eden. He missed that fellowship with the Lord. He was naked and ashamed, in the presence of the Lord, you can be transparent and open. You never have to wear fig leaves again. Fellowship gives us access to the throne of God.

CONSECRATION

day set aside for consecration is going to be vital as having the proper amount of blood in your body. This is what separated Israel from the world. Some situations will not change without it. The disciples asked Jesus, "Why could we not cast out a demon?" Some things come by fasting and praying. Fasting denies the flesh to his appetites and desires. It brings your soul (mind, will, and emotions) under control. The hearing becomes clearer. If it is done properly, it will revive and refresh you.

I set a goal to lose some excess weight. My sights were on joining a gym. I had dropped the ball when it came to regular fasting. The Lord reminded me of how vital it was for the ministry of deliverance he called me to. I am a pastor and an entrepreneur, so, scheduling my time is vital for me to remain balanced. Many of my business ventures turn into ministry. I am not so rigid that God cannot change my plans.

REST

There is a rest for the children of God, where they abstain from their labor. There are times we must find rest, by going to the other side like Jesus did so often in his ministry. Admitting that I can not accomplish alone what I may have, when I was younger without assistance. It takes teamwork to make a dream work. Jethro saw that the workload was overwhelming for Moses, so he chose seventy elders to help him from among-st the Israelites. Before you drown in responsibilities, ask for the help you need. Ask God to show the king your countenance, like Nehemiah and He will summon the help you need. He received enough help and supplies to finish we wall in fifty-two days. The Father wants the same from us. Ask and it shall be given unto you. Acknowledge you need help. God will send you the help you need. Know you can't do it by yourself.

STAND

*T*aking a stand sometimes means you will stand alone. Remind yourself that people are flesh and blood. People can be the toughest thing you have to overcome. It may not be the personality but the opinions of men. Turn your weapons on the real enemy which are principalities, rulers of darkness, and spiritual wickedness in high places with hidden agendas. Your knees may be buckling, and your teeth may be chattering. Stand even if you are afraid. This scripture has been my anchor. "Whenever I am afraid I will trust in you." (Psalms 56:3). You will have to stand through storms and pain. The weapons of our warfare are mighty through God for pulling down strongholds. Never allow the opinions of men to override the highest. They must do one or two things: respect or resent you. There is too much dumbing down in the body of Christ. There should be a difference in standards with the church. You will never win the world if you want to be like them. Standing is not about your two legs holding you up but a mindset that you are taking. You're not willing to compromise with anyone. Soldiers of the cross, I encourage you to stand and don't take down in this hour. We are not standing alone.

COURAGE

It takes courage to walk out of anything that has held you in bondage for years. People have invisible ropes on them that they are unaware of, and it's not until they are trying to break free that they begin to see how deep in the mud they have gotten themselves into. Courage will rise at the most critical times in your life. Fearful people find out what's inside of them when faced with life-or-death situations. Sometimes the person must become enraged to get the nerves they need to do something about a situation. Others must be encouraged enough to see it's going to take more than what they are presently doing to get an answer. Hope fuels courage because without it, men's hearts will fail. Hype does not produce the courage you need to stay with the assignment on your life. We need the truth of God's Word and activation of faith working in our heart. Every battle takes a different level of courage. David had a different level when he went up against Goliath. Courage brings giants down. Samson had courage even being blinded; he brought down the house. Courage subdues nations. God has not given us the spirit of fear. He does give us courage.

INDIRECT

I'm a very direct person, so it takes a whole lot of honesty to be that way. I have found that being this way sometime causes others to shy away. Christians should never approach anything in directly; this is when compromise would take place. Lies will be told, and the message you want to convey would not be understood. The Word says that you shall know the truth, and the truth shall make you free. Direct people are like black coffee; everybody doesn't drink it that way. You will find yourself in the class all your own. Invites will be redirected because of this trait. People will avoid you if possible.

Samuel was a direct prophet in the Bible. When he came to town, the people feared what the Lord had to say. Samuel would cut right to the chase. Nathan was a similar prophet. When King David told him of a dream, Nathan's reply was, "You are the man." Being indirect can cause you to lose your direction. Indirect people are easily taken on alternative routes. God does not want us to be double-minded nor does He wants us tossed to and fro by every wind and doctrine. Be direct and clear about things. Cast the vision and make it plain so the people can run with it.

BUILD

After the foundation is poured, hardened, and settled, then you can build a house. People with good foundations can be built upon. You can introduce them to new things, and they will run with it. A house with a good that foundation can stand through any type of weather. The materials that are used to build will matter. I am reminded of the three pigs. The house of straw could be blown down because of, words spoken to me to clout my decision making process. The house of sticks could be blown down by the reactions from others which sent my emotions on a roller coaster ride. The house of bricks was one that couldn't be destroyed.

Don't underestimate fragile people; they can become God's fatal weapons. God can take them and teach them life lessons in those broken places that will school them for a lifetime. This is not like Humpty Dumpty. God has a plan for the brokenhearted. He is close to you no matter how tiny the pieces of your heart are broken into. He can put you back together again. It will be as if nothing ever happened. Make sure your anchor holds and it is on a solid foundation.

SUPPORT

*T*he Lord will strongly support the righteous. He will also have people in your life that act like support beams. True support does more and talks less. People throw the word *love* around like a ball. *Love* is a verb and many still use it in the form of a noun. The Bible says to love thy neighbor as thyself. However you would like to be treated, treat others accordingly.

Our nation is under a pandemic while I'm writing this book. Everyone needs support one way or another. Helping and supporting have two different meanings. Anyone will help you for a while, then they will get weary in well doing. Support will be around for the duration. You can't tell support that's enough because you didn't call for the support. The Lord hired them, and He retires them. You notice I didn't say "fired" them. He sends them to another assignment to help God's people. When we call on the Lord in prayer for assistance, He summons them. There have been many things that I have been doing in maintaining two buildings. I often call on the Lord for assistance. I have a dear classmate who is always there for me. The Word tells us to be careful how we entertain strangers, for they could be angels of the unaware.

I remember as we were renovating our MLK location, one night, about two o'clock in the morning, he walked to my house which was about six blocks. He knocked on my door, and my husband answered. He said water had flooded the streets from the building, and he managed to turn it off outside. He wanted me to look inside to see if the water heater or a pipe had burst. Thankfully, this was not the problem.

On another occasion, I had to replace the flooring, and the existing flooring was going to be quite a challenge. He gave me some good advice after looking at it. He said, "I don't mind helping you do anything, but I believe there is a flooring you can put over this." I didn't see a person the streets had labeled; I saw my classmate who was on top in grade average in our class. I remembered his father being an educator and the first Black to own his own trailer park.

I said to him, "Do people realize if your father had to repair anything in these trailers, he probably taught you how?" I have many friends like this because what society calls an outcast, Jesus calls them friends. He supports me to this day. I have also found in times when I am doing a task that takes the strength of three men, God himself has aided me with supernatural strength, that the task would become easy. Support holds things up for periods of time. Help is temporary. We need to support one another.

UNDERSTANDING

$\mathcal{I}$ told the congregation that this year I was on a journey of discovering myself and getting to know who I was. This is vital when you are called to anything significant for God. This helps you to embrace the gifts and talents He has bestowed upon you. You will exercise your faith without wavering. Miracles, signs, and wonders will follow the Word. I often tell people that if you don't believe in yourself, how will you convince others to believe in you? We must get an understanding in all things. Have you ever seen someone put together a shelf without reading instructions? Many people try to do the will of God without reading His Word. They are putting together the current shelf based on the last shelf they constructed.

Every leader is different. If you had a good or bad relationship with that individual, don't assume this will be similar. No job is the same; it may be the same type of work, but they may have a different method of doing things. Assumption can be dangerous, especially if you think you know an individual. No relationship can't deepen if you don't spend time with the other. I can't possibly know my husband after fifteen minutes of fellowship. Yet we say we know God and seldom spend quality time with Him.

Jesus taught the disciples in parables. He took earthly things and compared them to spiritual things. There were times when the disciples took Him aside and asked Him what He meant. I had a parishioner say something so profound one day. Many people listen, but they don't hear. Faith comes by hearing the Word. What you hear, you get the understanding so you can act upon it. I often listen to different people say they heard from the Lord. I wait to see if the word they heard is going to be acted upon. Then there's another word from Him again. Soon you will end up with a big honey-do list and nothing accomplished on it. Understanding can bring people together, without it much will not get accomplished. A lot of important things hinges on understanding for your vision to be carried out. Things must be made plain (understandable) for people to run with it. Before you begin to blame others for their lack of assistance, make sure you have given them a good understanding of what you want.

This recent pandemic, with so much information coming from different directions, has imparted fear in so many. You may stock up on supplies and forget to wash your hands. It is important who you listen to, and it should be a trusted voice. Solomon said it best. Consider the whole matter. All I wanted to do was witness to others after receiving the gift of the Holy Spirit. This is the power afforded to the believer to empower them to be change agents for the kingdom of God. I remember telling my coworker that I would get a mic and preach on the streets if the Lord filled me. That was my first assignment as a street evangelist for over fifteen plus years. I don't expect all leaders to read this book. If you have a copy in your hand right now, the Lord can transform your life. "Therefore, if any man be in Christ, he is a new creature: old things are passed away; behold all things are become new" (2 Cor. 5:17).

GENDER REVEAL

This is the new form of introducing the sex of your baby to family and friends. The core theme of this book is to encourage female co-laborers in the gospel. There are times you must do a gender reveal. I'm not trying to be masculine nor am I trying to take anyone's place in the kingdom. You can be an evangelist, missionary, or emcee without any problems. The minute you say, "I'm a minister of the gospel," this is absurd in some areas. I have resolved not to seek a platform for a moment when I can build one to stand on for a lifetime. I've been in areas where they don't know how to address you, so they say nothing instead. I have witnessed sneers and laughter, only to have the last laugh. Women have always played a major role in the Bible. I don't think the Lord is going to take us out. Paul encouraged the Philippians to help, "And I entreat them also true yoke fellow, help those women which labored with me in the gospel, with Clement also both with my other fellow laborers, whose names are in the book of life" (Philippians 4:3 KJV) Moses was a prophet, but Miriam was a prophetess. Despite her error, she made a comeback and led the women in song and dance after crossing the Red Sea. Embrace your femininity and encourage other women to be all they can be in God. Women sometimes act worse than the opposite sex. They allow jealousy and competition to stop them from helping their sisters and brothers.

IT'S BEEN DROWNED

These have been the most critical times for me in this season. Despite all the interruptions and distractions, the Lord had caused me to finish strong, just as the last Israelite passed over. Moses stretched out his rod, and the Red Sea closed, drowning the Egyptians. Your past can't stop you anymore. The details about it can not haunt you either. It's been drowned. Sometimes there are victims of drownings that are never found. I believe that if you truly let go of the hurt, bitterness, and unforgiveness from unjust dealings, it will not resurface again. The Word says the Lord casts our sins as far as the east is from the west, and He remembers them no more. This is the key. Use your memory as a sea, and drown those negative thoughts. Think on things that are pure, lovely, just, and of a good report.

Moses is dead. The fearful, inadequate, and incapable person I thought I was is dead. I believe this book has been like a pouring out of a drink offering of the Lord; in turn, He takes my empty cup and fills it with good things. I was drowning and the Lord rescued me from the hand of the enemy. Moses allowed the people to define him and forgot all about his burning bush experience.

Joshua has arisen on the inside of me, and God has given me His courage. Now I know why the Lord told Joshua so many times be of a good courage. He didn't want him to forget in times of conquest. Tell someone today they can make it and you believe in them. It can make such a difference in their lives. Men need affirmation, and women need affection. When these needs are not met, a person will be lacking. God's job is to fulfill our spiritual needs, but He has let the natural responsibility on us. Do your part to make another person's life easier. Moses came as the deliverer for the Israelites. Who knows if you were brought to the kingdom for such a time as this? A deliverer can't be selfish but must be a servant. They mustn't fear but have faith. They must be a leader of people and a follower of God.

ABOUT THE AUTHOR

*A*ngela Clark is a philanthropist in her own right when it comes to her passion for encouraging people from all walks of life to go after their dreams until they have come to fruition.

Dr. Angela J. Clark
One Accord Outreach Int'l Church
Founder of Operation Love Outreach Ministries, Inc.